Let Me Tell You
About My Mom

photography *by* Ron Hayes

written by Casey Rislov *with* Ron Hayes

Mountain Stars Press • Wyoming • USA

Dear grownups,

Let Me Tell You About My Mom is structured to be enjoyed with children of all ages, from the littlest listeners to older kids who are ready for more detailed information about animals, or who are beginning to read themselves. You can read just the introductory text on each page to younger children and include the expository text for older kids. For the very youngest listeners, you can enjoy the book as a simple picture book, pointing to the large, colorful name of each animal, and then ask questions about what's happening in the pictures: What color are the animals? Are they big or small? What are they doing? How many babies do you see?

Enjoy the book in any way that works for you and *your* babies.

Text and images copyright © 2023 Ron Hayes
The burrowing owl in flight was used with permission from
award-winning photographer Scott Wilson (wilsonaxpe.com).
The nuzzling moose image was used with permission from photographer Heath Hayes.
Design by Lois Rainwater

Mountain Stars Press
caseyrislovbooks@gmail.com
www.caseyrislovbooks.com

Printed in China
First Edition
10 9 8 7 6 5 4 3 2 1
LCCN 2022913718
ISBN 979-8-218-04484-8

book bridge press

This book was proudly produced by Book Bridge Press
www.bookbridgepress.com

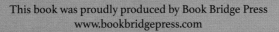

To my husband, Chris, and my boys, Alex and Asher—
you are my favorite thing about every day.
—C. R.

This book was inspired by all the mothers in my life. First,
my mother Lily, who supported me in everything that I
have been fortunate enough to do in life,
and who allowed me to grow up wild in Wyoming's
wide-open spaces, as her mother and her
mother's mother did before her.
My wife Kristie, the mother of my fifth-
generation Wyomingites, who helped me
raise three wildlings of our own.
My daughter Faith, who made me a
grandfather and ushered in generation
number six with her son Kylo. And my
daughter Adeah, who has yet to start but
will have a family of her own someday soon.
And a special thank-you to my late father
Leroy and my son Heath,
who has accompanied me on many
adventures, and who contributed a
moose image to this book.
— R. H.

Mamas take good care of their babies. Animal mamas take good care of their babies too! Mamas feed their babies and later teach them how to feed themselves. They keep their babies warm and safe. However, there are difficulties raising young in the wild. Mothers must teach their young how to thrive and survive in a very wild world.

Let's meet some animal mamas and learn how they take care of their babies.

Brown Bears

Mama brown bears take good care of their cubs. Our mom watches us roll around and wrestle in the tall grass. Play is fun, but it also teaches us how to defend ourselves and how to find food.

North American brown bears are large bears, but mama teaches her cubs to find some of the smallest bites of food. When the tides go out, brown bears wander the ocean flats and sniff clams under the sand. When Mama Bear finds one, she digs it up and uses her long claws to open the clams before giving her cubs the salty treats found inside.

Loons

Mama loons take good care of their chicks. My mom has some of the most unusual eyes in nature. They help her find food underwater. She is my protector, provider, and comforter.

For the first several days of life, loon chicks cannot regulate their own body temperatures (thermoregulation). They can swim, but after being in the cold northern waters for too long, they must get out and ride on their mothers' warm backs. When it is time for the mom to feed her chicks, she will "dump" them into the water by lowering herself or by raising up and stretching her wings, causing the chicks to gently fall into the water.

The chicks are fed a steady diet of insect larvae, nymphs, crayfish, and small fish until they are old enough to feed themselves, usually at about two months of age.

Mama swift foxes take good care of their kits. My mom made our den full of multiple entrances and exits so we can weather a storm or dodge an unwanted stranger. When we are outside under the big sky, my mom watches over us while we hunt and play.

Swift foxes come by their names naturally. Just a few weeks after birth, they are already one of the fastest animals on the plains. Every game their mom plays with her kits is to teach them how to hunt and survive. The kits are nimble and fierce in their play, but Mom's temper tells the kits when it's time to stop. She allows her kits to try new things and take risks, but she lets the kits know when they take it too far.

Swift Foxes

Mountain Goats

Nothing beats living on top of the mountain peaks, and few other creatures can withstand the conditions. But mountain goats are well suited for high mountain living. The cloven hooves and rough pads on their feet allow them to climb and leap with their fearless mother anywhere. Their rambunctious ways are not for the faint of heart, as their horns are as sharp as the rocky terrain where they live and play.

Mama mountain goats take good care of their kids. We already live where most will not go, so Mom makes sure we stay safe wherever we are on our journey.

Mama black bears take good care of their cubs. My mom is strong and powerful, but she is also a gentle teacher. She shows me how to use my nose to find the ripest berries.

In the first year and a half, black bear cubs learn through their mother that their amazing bodies help them find food. Their noses are their super-power, helping them smell danger as well as food. Cubs use their claws for play and to search for food in leafy limbs. Endlessly curious, bear cubs find trouble easily and keep their mother very busy!

Black Bears

Mama bobcats take good care of their kittens. My mom watches and listens to keep us safe. She does not miss anything we do.

Mama bobcats are skillful hunters. They may look relaxed, but they are always watching and listening, noticing every movement and creature big or small. They can bound in a single leap to protect their kittens. Mamas teach their kittens how to hunt during dawn and dusk, showing them how to jump, chase, ambush, and hide. She also lets her kittens play with each other to practice these skills.

Bobcats

Mama cow elk take good care of their calves. In our herd, Mom is the boss. We travel with family and friends, but I can always feel the warmth of my mom as she nestles me close.

Cow Elk

Cow elk are matriarchal, which means that female cows lead the way. The older and wiser cows look for safe pathways to travel, and they alert the herd when danger approaches. Cow elk are very vocal, and calves must learn what each sound means. Mama cows may mew just to tell her calves where she is, but when Papa Elk bugles, he shows his calves when it is time to get out of the way.

Badgers

Mama badgers take good care of their badger cubs. Most know that my mom can be strong and fierce, but she can be just as tender. She snuggles us safe in our den.

The badger is mostly nocturnal, meaning they are active at night. They have large front claws that make them amazing diggers for finding food and creating dens. Badger cubs stay with their mom in their den for about eight to ten weeks. They become totally independent after five or six months.

Pronghorns

Mama pronghorn take good care of their fawns. After I am born, my mother will keep me hidden from danger. She protects me by keeping a close watch over me until my eyes and legs are as strong as hers.

Pronghorn are the fastest land animal in North America. Their powerful eyes and swift feet are well suited for the open land where they live. Pronghorn have large eyes that can see eight times more effectively than a human! Pronghorn fawns' legs grow strong by keeping up with their mom. Sometimes they run just for fun. It is what pronghorn were made to do.

Mama deer take good care of their fawns. When we are born, we have no scent and Mom keeps her distance to make sure we stay safe in the prairie grasses and brush.

Deer live and grow in many environments, which allows them to try many different seasonal foods. Deer are herbivores, which means they eat only plants. They can even get their water from pounding leaves with their hooves. Deer have great night vision, which helps them see and avoid all the predators they may encounter.

Deer

Moose

Mama moose take good care of their calves. I am safest at my mother's side. She comforts me and teaches me which foods will help me grow.

Moose are born in the spring. They have very long legs that make them a bit clumsy. Mama Moose will show her calves how to use their legs to their advantage. She teaches her calves where to go and where not to go, helping them navigate the willows and move effortlessly through the water's edge. Mother moose are fiercely protective of their calves and can be dangerous for any other creature that wishes her calf harm.

Mama burrowing owls take good care of their owlets. My mom and dad work as a team to protect and take care of me. They will defend me and my nest, and they bring me bugs to eat.

Burrowing Owls

Even as adults, burrowing owls are small birds, but mama owls are very capable of protecting their young. When they think they are in danger, owls hide in their burrows and make sounds to mimic rattlesnakes. They also bob their heads up and down, and might scream, cluck, or chatter to protect their nests.

Their burrows are underground and are often the former burrows of other animals such as prairie dogs, rabbits, or snakes.

There are so many ways animal mamas take good care of their babies. Mamas keep constant watch over their young to keep them safe from danger so their babies can thrive in their new worlds in any season. Animal mamas teach their babies how to use their bodies for survival. This includes finding food, seeking shelter, and learning how to stay safe.

After working hard all day to learn new skills, it's time for all sleepy babies to rest and snuggle with their mamas.

RON HAYES is a wildlife photographer and filmmaker.
He resides in Wyoming where his family has been since the late 1800s.
He has a degree in wildlife biology, and this knowledge base allows him
to capture behaviors on camera that most would never notice.
See more of Ron's work at westernwildlifeimages.com and on
the *Wild and Exposed* podcast at wildandexposed.com
and the *Wild and Exposed* podcast channel on YouTube.

CASEY RISLOV treasures time with her family in the wide-open spaces of the West.
Her sons' curiosity is wilder than the wildlife on these grand adventures,
and her Mother's Day gifts have included rocks, squirmy worms, and even a
horned toad. Casey Rislov has a bachelor's degree in biology from
the University of Wyoming and a master's degree in education
from Montana State University.